Please Help Me Wi

MW01518897

Homework Strategies for Parents and Caregivers

Susan Gingras Fitzell, M.Ed.

Cogent Catalyst Publications

Fitzell, Susan Gingras
    Please Help Me With My Homework! Strategies for Parents and Caregivers 85 pp.
ISBN 1-932995-04-8

_____

For Information, address:

Susan Gingras Fitzell
Cogent Catalyst Publications
PO Box 6182
Manchester, NH 03108-6182
603-625-6087

For more information email:
info@cogentcatalyst.com
www.cogentcatalyst.com
www.aimhieducational.com

For supplemental handouts and information:
www.aimhieducational.com/inclusion.html

Other selected titles by Susan Gingras Fitzell, M.Ed.

Special Needs in the General Classroom: Strategies to Make it Work
Free the Children: Conflict Education for Strong Peaceful Minds

Transforming Anger to Personal Power: An Anger Management Curriculum Guide for Grades 6 through 12

DEDICATION

To Ian, who taught me how to teach at home.

Special thanks to Monica Marcotte and Dawn Sorli for your editing contributions. You've helped me to be clear with my instructions so that readers will be successful using these strategies.

Introduction

Recent scientific research has confirmed that we all have different learning preferences and that we all learn best with different strategies. Brain research has shown that regardless of learning style, we all process information in specific ways. This book provides the reader with simple, proven tools to help children increase academic performance and make the homework experience more rewarding and productive.

With researched examples and processes that have been proven to be successful in the classroom, this book offers useful tools that help your child succeed at any grade level.

For the sake of reading ease, I may refer to him, her, your child, youth, student, randomly. I realize that you, the reader, might be working with a brother, sister, foster child, neighbor, grandchild, your own child, etc. Some of you may even be working with college level students, or adult learners. I hope that the way that I have chosen to refer to the "person being helped with homework" respects all possible relationships.

Thank you for purchasing this book. I would love feedback on what you try that works or what would make this book even better. I would love to hear from you.

Susan Fitzell

How the Brain Learns

How We Learn According to Brain Research

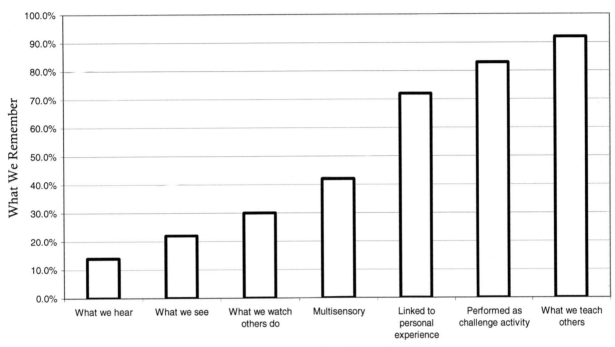

Sources:

Dryden, Gordon. Voss, Jeannette. <u>The Learning Revolution: A Life-Long Learning Program for the World's Finest Computer Your Amazing Brain</u>. Rolling Hills Estates: Jalmar Press, 1994.

Glasser, William. <u>Control Theory in the Classroom</u>. 1st ed. Perennial Library, 1986.

Multiple Intelligence / Learning Style

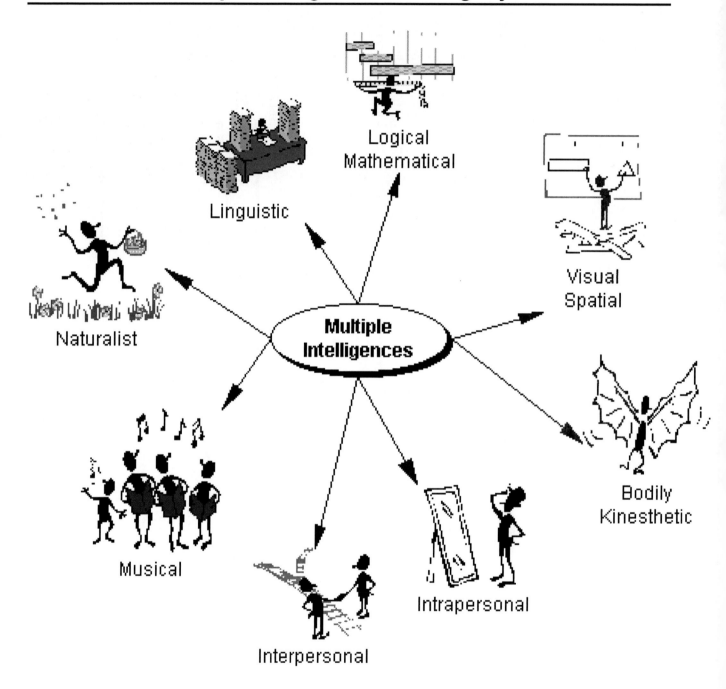

Linguistic

Logical
Mathematical

Visual
Spatial

Naturalist

**Multiple
Intelligences**

Bodily
Kinesthetic

Musical

Interpersonal

Intrapersonal

Assessment Checklist for Multiple Intelligence / Learning Style

Instructions

Read the checklists on the following pages to determine your learning style. Put a checkmark near the bullets that describe how you learn best. The boxes that have the most checks may indicate the type of learner that you are. This is not a test. It is simply a tool to start thinking about how you might learn best. Use the strategy pages following this assessment for study suggestions. Try them. If it works for you, keep doing it! If it does not work, try something else.

Linguistic	Logical-Mathematical
<ul><li>Tells tall tales, jokes and stories</li><li>Has a good memory</li><li>Enjoys word games</li><li>Enjoys reading and writing</li><li>Has a good vocabulary for his/her age</li><li>Has good verbal communication</li><li>Enjoys crossword puzzles</li><li>Appreciates nonsense rhymes, puns, tongue twisters, etc.</li><li>Spells words accurately (or if preschool, spells using sounds that are advanced for age)</li></ul>	<ul><li>Asks questions about how things work</li><li>Enjoys math activities</li><li>Enjoys playing chess, checkers, or other strategy games</li><li>Enjoys logic puzzles or brain teasers</li><li>Uses higher-order thinking skills</li><li>Interested in patterns, categories and relationships</li><li>Likes doing and creating experiments</li><li>Does arithmetic problems in his or her head quickly (or if preschool, math concepts are advanced for age)</li><li>Has a good sense of cause and effect</li></ul>
Bodily Kinesthetic	**Spatial**
<ul><li>Excels in one or more sports or physical arts</li><li>Moves, twitches, taps or fidgets while seated for a long time</li><li>Enjoys taking things apart and putting them back together</li><li>Touches new objects</li><li>Enjoys running, jumping or wrestling</li><li>Expresses him or herself dramatically</li><li>Enjoys modeling clay and finger painting</li><li>Good with his or her hands</li><li>Cleverly mimics other people's gestures or mannerisms</li><li>Reports different physical sensations while thinking or working</li></ul>	<ul><li>Daydreams more than peers</li><li>Enjoys art activities</li><li>Likes visual presentations</li><li>Enjoys puzzles and mazes</li><li>Understands more from pictures than words while reading</li><li>Doodles on paper</li><li>Loves construction sets: Legos, K'nex, Capsela, etc.</li><li>Often inventing things</li><li>Draws things that are advanced for age</li><li>Reads maps, charts, and diagrams more easily than text (or if preschool, enjoys looking at more than text)</li></ul>

Musical	Interpersonal
<ul><li>Recognizes off-key music</li><li>Remembers melodies</li><li>Plays a musical instrument or sings in a choir.</li><li>Speaks or moves rhythmically</li><li>Taps rhythmically as he or she works</li><li>Is sensitive to environmental noise</li><li>Responds favorably to music</li><li>Sings songs that he or she has learned outside of the classroom</li><li>Is a discriminating listener</li><li>Creates his or her own songs and melodies</li></ul>	<ul><li>Enjoys socializing with peers</li><li>Acts as a natural leader</li><li>Gives advice to friends who have problems</li><li>Seems to be street-smart</li><li>Belongs to clubs, committees, or other organizations</li><li>Likes to play games with other kids</li><li>Has one or more close friends</li><li>Shows concern for others</li><li>Perceives and makes distinctions in people's moods, intentions and motivations</li><li>Good at responding to other people's feelings</li></ul>
Intrapersonal	**Naturalist**
<ul><li>Displays a sense of independence or a strong will</li><li>Has a realistic sense of his or her strengths</li><li>Has a good sense of self-direction</li><li>Prefers working alone to working with others, may be shy</li><li>Learns from his or her failures and successes</li><li>Is insightful and self-aware</li><li>Adapts well to his or her environment</li><li>Is aware of own emotions, strengths, and limitations</li><li>Is self-disciplined</li><li>Marches to the beat of different drummer in his/her style of living and learning</li></ul>	<ul><li>Enjoys labeling and identifying nature</li><li>Sensitive to changes in weather</li><li>Good at distinguishing among cars, sneakers, and jewelry, etc.</li></ul>

Suggestions for Learning According to Multiple Intelligence

We learn through all intelligence styles, we just have some learning preferences that are stronger than others are. Choose strategies that support your strongest learning preference.

For Verbal/Linguistic Learners

These learners learn by saying, hearing, and seeing words. They can easily memorize names, dates, places, and trivia. To help verbal/linguistic learners:

- Use descriptive language
- Have them study by reading, writing, telling stories, playing word games, and working with jokes and riddles.
- They are good at creating imaginary worlds.
- Create crossword puzzles for practice at www.puzzlemaker.com

For Logical Mathematical Learners

These learners are adept at categorizing, classifying, and working with abstract patterns and relationships. They work well with reasoning, numbers, abstractions, logic, and problem solving, and moving from the concrete to the abstract.

- Compare and contrast ideas
- Create a time line
- Classify concepts/objects/materials
- Read or design maps
- Use a Venn diagram to explain…
- Teach using technology

For Body Kinesthetic Learners

The brain's motor cortex, which controls bodily motion, is the key to the intelligence of bodily/kinesthetic learners. These learners need to touch, move, interact with space, and process knowledge through bodily sensations.

- Create hands on projects
- Conduct hands on experiments
- Create human sculptures to illustrate situations
- Re-enact great moments from history
- Make task or puzzle cards for …

For Visual Spatial Learners

Visual/spatial learners rely on their sense of sight and ability to visualize an object. They create mental images and learn by drawing, building, and designing. Encourage use of color in their work.

- Make visual organizer or memory model of the material being learned.
- Graph the results of a survey or results from a course of study.
- Create posters or flyers
- Create Collages
- Draw Maps
- Color-code the process of…

For Musical Rhythmic Learners

Musical/rhythmic learners recognize tonal patterns. For optimal learning, suggest they hum or sing information they want to grasp, or have them move their bodies while they study.

- Create "raps" (key dates, math, and poems) or write new lyrics to a song so that it explains...
- Identify social issues through lyrics
- Analyze different historical periods through their music
- Make up sounds for different math operations or processes
- Use music to enhance the learning of...

For Interpersonal Learners

Person-to-person relationships and communication are necessary for interpersonal learners. They study and work best with others.

- Analyze relationships in a story
- Review a material/concepts/books orally
- Discuss/debate controversial issues
- Find relationships between objects, cultures, situations
- Role-play a conversation with an important historical figure
- Solve complex word problems in a group
- Peer Tutor the subject being learned

For Intrapersonal Learners

Almost the exact opposite of interpersonal learners, intrapersonal learners thrive by working alone. Self-paced instruction and individualized projects work best with these students. Suggest that intrapersonal learners keep a daily journal, as their thoughts are directed inward. They have a great degree of self-understanding and they rely deeply on their instincts.

- Keep a journal to demonstrate learning
- Analyze historical personalities
- Imagine self as character in history, or scientist discovering a cure, or mathematician working a theory and describe or write about what you imagine to demonstrate learning

For Naturalist Learners

Naturalist learners observe and understand the organized patterns in the natural environment. Provide them with visualization activities and hands-on activities that are based on nature. Bring the outdoors into their learning whenever possible. Study in ways that call on the naturalist learner's abilities to measure, map, and chart observations of plants and animals.

- Sort and classify content in relation to the natural world
- Interact with nature through field trips
- Encourage learning in natural surroundings
- Categorize facts about...

Strategies for Setting Up a Homework Environment

- Provide a comfortable place to work without distractions.
- If possible, use full spectrum lighting.
- Calm the homework beast with music at 60 beats /minute or less
    - Helps with attention issues and sensory processing
    - Supports organized body movement
    - Assists active engagement of the learner
    - Increases the brain's alpha and beta waves which are associated with a quiet alert state ready for learning
    - Helps to provide structure for organized thinking, e.g. Writing reports or papers, activities that involve planning

Music suggestions:
- Native American Flute
- Peruvian Mantra
- Mozart for Learning (Caution: Some Classical is too rambunctious. The key is 60 beats per minute or less.)
- Enya
- Typically, music without words that might be sung (and therefore distracting.)

You might also check the beat of the music with the second had of your watch or clock.

Paper & Pencil Strategies

- Have children print information to be memorized.
- Border key spelling words, people, places, etc.
- Have children use two colors when working alternating the color of each fact they are writing in their notes. Color makes facts stand out as unique. If all notes are in one color, nothing stands out as unique and is therefore harder to remember.
    - Highlight
    - Alternate color gel pens, markers, crayons, etc.
- Border key spelling words, people, places, etc. See example below.

For more information about color and memory, see page 33.

Mind & Body Connection Strategies

- Use movement to enhance memory.
    - Act out vocabulary words.
    - Come up with a gesture to represent key people, places, or things.
    - Use sign language.
    - Basketball spelling:
        - If you have a hoop in your driveway, yard, or neighborhood, make a game out of spelling a word then shooting a basket. It does not matter what rules you make up. The movement, fun, and challenge in the activity are what is important.
        - If you like football, soccer or any other sports better, use that sport as the foundation. Make your own rules. As long as spelling, etc. is part of the game rules, it will be effective.
    - Hop & Chunk Spelling.
        - Break a word into spelling "chunks" and hop while spelling each chunk.
        E.g.: Maneuver
        Man (hop) eu (hop) ver (hop)

Vocabulary Study Strategy

1. Choose a vocabulary word.
2. Print it on one side of a "flash" card. (Use index cards, heavy paper cut into strips, etc.)
3. border it.
4. Ask your child to tell you what he or she thinks it means so that it draws from what your child already knows.
5. Reinforce the correct definition.
6. Print the definition on the other side of the "flash" card.
7. Stand and act out a movement for the word while spelling it aloud three times!

Start the process over with the next word on the spelling or vocabulary list.

If your child's teacher requires that he or she write the words three times each in cursive, ask the teacher if your child can write the word two times in cursive and one time printed on a flash card. Explain that you are better able to help your child with flash cards. Some children will not mind writing the words four times each. My children, however, objected to the extra work and even insisted, "But the teacher says I have to do it THIS way!" So, I made a deal with the teacher to have one set of words on flash cards and the teacher told my child that it was Okay.

Brain Gym® - Kinesthetic Strategy

BRAIN GYMNASTICS: A Wakeup Call to the Brain[1]

Brain Gym® is a series of exercises that enables the brain to work at its best. The techniques are a composite of many differing sciences predominantly based upon neurobiology. It has been found to facilitate learning in learning-disabled children. However, the results of using Brain Gym(R) have proven to be highly effective for all learners. There is even evidence that Brain Gym(R) can be used for psychological disorders as well.

Teachers will find these exercises enhance student performance before test taking in particular, but also they work before listening to lectures and studying. It also may relieve stress.

How does it work? Carla Hannaford, Ph.D., neurophysiologist, states in "Smart Moves." that our bodies are very much a part of all our learning, and learning is not an isolated "brain" function. Every nerve and cell is a network contributing to our intelligence and our learning capability. She states, "Movement activates the neural wiring throughout the body, making the whole body the instrument of learning". Carla states that "sensation" forms the basis of concepts from which "thinking" evolves.

Brain Gym® exercises consider our bi-cameral brain. The brain has a left and a right hemisphere, each one performing distinct tasks. Often one side of our brain works more than the other depending upon the tasks we are

---

[1] Adapted from an article by Ruth Trimble (trimble@hawaii.edu)

Much of the factual material for this article is taken from "Smart Moves" by Carla Hannaford, Ph.D. and Dr. Paul Dennison and his EduK(R) literature. Please cite these authors when using this material. Permission to use my data is given, but it constitutes only my opinion and limited practical experience and is not in any way intended to represent the official Brain Gym(R) or EduK(R) view nor to give permission to reproduce the detailed exercises designed by the other authors without citing them.

doing or on how we have developed as human beings. If the two hemispheres are working fully and sharing information across the corpus callosum, then there is a balance of brain function. Without this balance, there is always going to be something that is not understood or remembered. Brain Gym® assists in integrating the two hemispheres, giving us full capacity for problem solving or learning.

We are also "electrical" beings and our brain's neurons work by electrical connections. Water has been found to be the best thing we can use to facilitate the thinking process because of its capacity to conduct electricity and assist cell function. As Carla Hannaford says, "Water comprises more of the brain (with estimates of 90%) than of any other organ of the body." Thus, a simple drink of water before a test or before going to class can have a profound effect on our brain's readiness to work. Unfortunately, coffee or soda will have the opposite effect since these will upset the electrolytes in the brain. In all, then the exercises that you see here are designed to make us a whole-brain learner. Following, are some simple but effective ways to wake-up the brain and get it all working at once and optimally. Before any of the following exercises, DRINK a glass of water.

BRAIN BUTTONS

This exercise helps the carotid arteries to open and function better in sending blood to the brain. It also helps lower blood pressure.

1. Put one hand so that there is as wide a space as possible between the thumb and index finger. Spread your hand apart, and then bring your four fingers together, leaving your thumb extended as far as possible from the index finger.
2. Then place your index and thumb into the slight indentations below the collarbone on each side of the sternum.
3. Press lightly in a pulsing manner.
4. At the same time put the other hand over the navel area of the stomach.
5. Gently press on these points for about 2 minutes.

CROSS CRAWL

This exercise assists the corpus callosum by forcing signals to pass between the brains and cross over the mid-point. The corpus callosum is the thick band of nerve fibers that connects the two hemispheres of the brain and allows the hemispheres to communicate.

1. You can stand or sit for this. Put the right hand across the body to the left knee as you raise it, and then do the same thing for the left hand on the right knee just as if you were marching.
2. Just do this either sitting or standing for about 2 minutes.

HOOK-UPS

This works well for nerves before a test or special event such as making a speech. Anytime there is nervousness or anxiety, this will calm.

1. Sit for this activity and cross the right leg over the left at the ankles.
2. Take your right wrist and cross it over the left wrist and link up the fingers so that the right wrist is on top.
3. Now bend the elbows out and gently turn the fingers in towards the body until they rest on the sternum (breastbone) in the center of the chest.
4. Stay in this position.
5. Touch your tongue to your palate.
6. Breathe in through your nose and out through your mouth in slow, deep, belly breaths.
7. Keep the ankles crossed and the wrists crossed and then breathe evenly in this position for a few minutes.
8. You will be noticeably calmer after that time.

Ruth Trimble states, "My student test scores have gone up because of Brain Gym®. I have children achieving far higher scores than I have seen using the same screening and testing methods for the past six years. The ones who are doing Brain Gym® are accomplishing so much more."

Teaching Each Other

- You and your child are partners.
- Set your timer for 1-2 minutes
- Ask your child to teach you one thing from the homework, what they learned in class today, etc.
- Set timer for 1-2 minutes.
- You re-teach your child one thing from their homework, class work, etc. (Something different from what they taught you. Choose from their study materials.)
- Repeat for one more round.

Music as a Strategy

The brain processes and remembers music differently than it processes and remembers spoken words and symbols. Using music to memorize information is a highly effective strategy that is seriously underutilized. Advertisers use music in product jingles to promote their products. They do it because the jingles cause us to "remember" their product when shopping. Parents can use this strategy with their children to help them memorize key information needed for tests, quizzes, and general knowledge. Children as young as two years old can be taught to remember their name address and phone number to music. Singing is a powerful memory tool.

- Link old tunes with new concepts
    - Sing the helping verbs to the tune of "Mary Had a Little Lamb".
    - Pick a popular song and rewrite the lyrics of the song to match the information to be memorized.
    - Rap it! Chant it! Clap it!

Here are some examples:
Quadratic equation to the tune of "Pop! Goes the Weasel"
x e-quals neg-a-tive b
plus or minus the squaaaare root
of b squared minus fouuur a c
all over twooo a

Helping verbs to the tune of "Mary Had a Little Lamb"
Is, are, was, were, am, be, been
Have, has, had
Do, did, does
May, might, mu-ust,
Can, will, shall, ...Could, would, should, being

Mind Mapping/Graphic Roadmaps/Visual Organizers

I started using mind mapping after reading *I Can See You Naked: a Fearless Guide to Making Great Presentations* by Ron Hoff (1988). My first presentation was drawn out like a colorful board game with a route to follow, arrows, and picture images of what I was going to do. I remember thinking how much easier it was to use than index cards with a text script written on them. It also was much less restricting. I did not feel tied to reading the cards. Rather, I looked at the picture and went from memory. It saved me from being tied to a script.

The technique worked so well for me that I started expanding the idea into my teaching efforts. **As I read selections from English texts to my students, I drew the events out on paper in map and graphic format.** I would interject silly ditties and exclamations of passion into the effort to make what I was reading to them stick out in their memory. Given my students were at the cool age of teen, they would often look at me and exclaim, "You are crazy!" and my pat answer was always, "Yes, I am, but you'll remember this because of it". Moreover, they did.

Children learn and remember mind maps better if they create them out of their own mental images and patterns. See examples below.

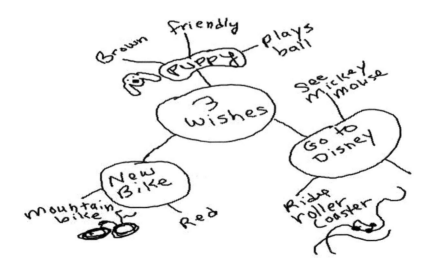

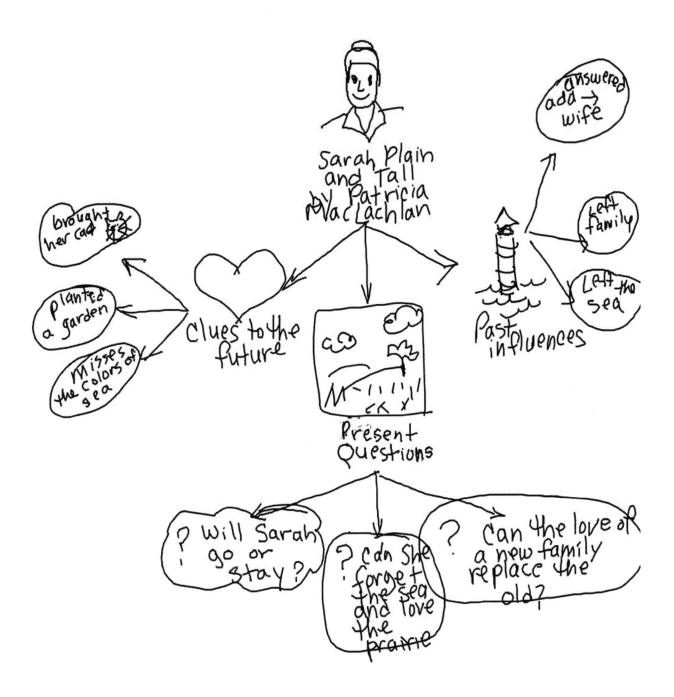

When children make spelling errors at this phase of the creative process, note them, but let them go. Correcting a child's spelling while they are creating will cause them to clutter their working memory with rules and not allow enough "space" for coming up with ideas. So, correct the difference between 'add' and 'ad' later.

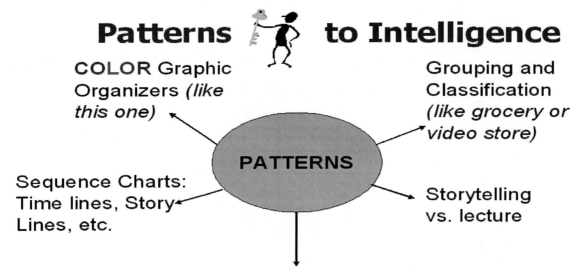

Patterns to Intelligence

COLOR Graphic Organizers *(like this one)*

Grouping and Classification *(like grocery or video store)*

Sequence Charts: Time lines, Story Lines, etc.

PATTERNS

Storytelling vs. lecture

Ask kids to find patterns: *cause and effect*, **problem and solution**, **intense drama and down time.**

Mnemonic Devices [2]

Mnemonic: n. A device, such as a formula or rhyme, used as an aid in remembering.

Mnemonics, or the science and art of aiding memory, is an ancient concept. Many people rely on mnemonic devices to help remember what they have learned or need to recall, from grocery lists to people's names to kings and queens or the presidents. What works for one person may not work for another. The following five memory devices help to improve retention of information.

Some examples of mnemonics:

- **I AM A PERSON**: The 4 Oceans (**In**dian, **A**rctic, **A**tlantic, **P**acific)
- HOMES: Huron, Ontario, Michigan, Erie, Superior: the Great Lakes in North America

The best are those made up by the student, as they are meaningful to him or her.

---

[2] Adapted from the work of Michael DiSpezio, author of *Critical Thinking Puzzles* (Sterling, 1996) for Scientific American Frontiers. http://www.pbs.org/saf/4_class/45_pguides/pguide_703/4573_trufalse.html

Associations

Developing associations is a familiar strategy used to recall information by connecting it to other, more familiar pieces of information.

For example, memorizing a sequence of seemingly random digits is easy when that number series is your birth date or street address.

Developing associations is also a helpful way to remember new information.

Rhyming

Rhymes and jingles are powerful memory devices. Just think how often you have used the rhyme, "Thirty days has September. . ." to recall the number of days within a month.

To use the Rhyme Technique all you have to do is make up a rhyme to remember what you want to remember! It is fun! If you are musically inclined, you can even make up whole songs to help you remember long pieces of important information.

Examples:
30 days has September
April, June, and November

In 1492, Columbus sailed the ocean blue.

In 1903, the Wright brothers flew free.
First successful flight

I before E except after C
And when saying "A" as in Neighbor or Weigh
And weird is weird.

Chunking

When reciting a telephone or Social Security number, most people are apt to speak it in three chunks. For example, the first and second chunks of a phone number consist of three digits and the third chunk contains four digits. Chunking the numbers makes a meaningless series easier to remember. Can you think of other series of numbers that are frequently chunked?

800-566-3712

Chunking is also an excellent strategy for remembering how to spell words. An example of chunking follows:

man EU ver

Other examples:
ALBU QUER QUE
RE NUMER ATION
PENN SYLVAN IA
CZ ECHO SLO VAKIA
LEU KE MIA
FRE NET IC
RECE IVE

Acronyms

An acronym is a word formed from the initial letter or letters of each of the parts of a name or organization.

For example:
LASER stands for Light Amplification by Stimulated Emission of Radiation.
REM sleep stands for Rapid Eye Movement.
NASA stands for National Aeronautical and Space Administration.
ZIP code stands for Zone Improvement Plan.

You can also make up acronyms to help you remember information. Think of an acronym as a "fun" word or phrase in which each letter stands for the first letter of the item to be recalled.

Acrostics

An acrostic is a memory strategy similar to an acronym, but it takes the first letters of a series of words, lines, or verses to form a memorable phrase. Sometimes the phrase is nonsense, which may help you remember it!

Here is one: King Philip Came Over For Grandma's Soup. Each acrostic stands for the biological classification hierarchy (Kingdom, Phylum, Class, Order, Family, Genus, and Species).

Example of mnemonics combined with meaningful pictures that use associations:

Taxonomy

King Philip Came Over For Grandma's Soup.
Kingdom Phylum Class Order Family Genus Species

© AIMHI Ed Programs

Use Adding Machine Tape to Remember Sequences

Use **adding machine tape** to create a visual storyline, time line, or sequence to be memorized.

Instructions:

As your child is reading through a textbook or story, they draw pictures of the important information (characters, historical figures, places, events, etc.) in the order that they read the information on adding machine tape.

For example, when you read about how the Lakota used directions, you draw a picture of it on the tape. Next the chapter describes what types of information was recorded such as position of the sun, of the moon, neighbor sites, etc. Draw and label that information in the same sequence/order that it is listed or described in the textbook. See below for examples.

Now, the student has a "time line" or "story line" in sequential order of the events in the textbook or story. This visual memory tool will help him/her to remember the information in the order that it "happened".

Color and Memory

Simply put, we remember what we see in color better than what we see in black and white. According to Eric Jensen in *Brain-Based Learning* (1996), we remember colors first and content next. Colors affect us on physiological and psychological levels.

- Add color to homework paperwork
- Print notes and alternate two colors for each individual point.
- Hang colorful posters to reinforce concepts being learned around the house.

According to the research, color communicates more effectively than black and white. How much more effectively? Here's what the research says:

- Color visuals increase willingness to read by up to 80 percent.[3]
- Using color can increase motivation and participation by up to 80 percent.[3]
- Color enhances learning and improves retention by more than 75 percent.[4]
- Color accounts for 60 percent of the acceptance or rejection of an object and is a critical factor in the success of any visual experience.[5]

The Meaning of Color

- Red - an engaging and emotive color, which can stimulate hunger or excite and disturb the individual.
- Yellow - the first color distinguished by the brain.
- Blue - Calms a tense person and increases feelings of well-being.
- Green - A calming color, like blue
- Brown - promotes a sense of security and relaxation and reduces fatigue.

---

[3] The Persuasive Properties of Color; Ronald E. Green; Marketing Communications, October 1984.
[4] Loyola University School of Business, Chicago, IL., as reported in Hewlett-Packard's Advisor, June 1999; (http://www.hpadvisor.com).
[5] The Power of Color; Dr. Morton Walker; Avery Publishing Group; 1991.

The Fitz-spell Method of Studying Spelling Words

Option 1:
Use phonics rules to determine which letters should be in a **standout color**.

These cards are actually done in color markers. All pictures used in this handbook were originally done in color.

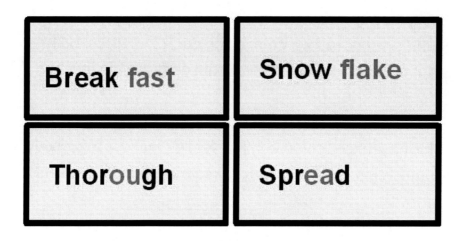

You might find the phonics rules by going to an internet search engine and typing in "phonics rules" or in a phonics book available at libraries and bookstores.

Option 2:

Pre-test
Use pre-test errors to determine which letters should be in a **standout color**.

Theory: Make the corrected mistake in spelling stand out so that the mistake is not repeated.

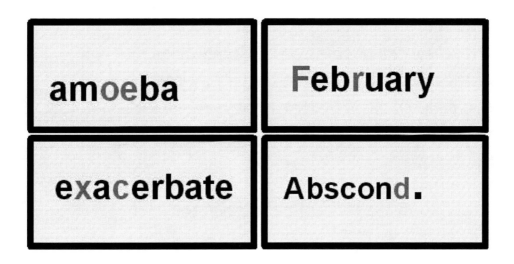

amoeba	February
exacerbate	Abscond.

1.   Whenever possible, add clip art pictures to 'visualize' the word.
2.   Use bright color markers with good contrast to differentiate.
3.   Add any other symbols, sound cues, etc. to make the spelling word more memorable.
4.   PRINT the words on INDEX CARDS.
5.   Practice by running through the cards 2-3 times each day for the four days before the spelling test. Put aside the cards that need more study. Cards that can be spelled quickly can be pulled out of the daily second and third run.

Good luck! You should see a significant improvement in spelling test grades.

Three Card Match: Review Strategy

Materials

- Index Cards
  - Choose three of the following card colors: pink, green, blue, yellow, or white.
  - If you only have white cards or white paper, color-code the cards. For example:
    - Put a yellow dot or stripe on the word cards.
    - Put a green dot or stripe on the picture cards.
    - Put a pink dot or stripe on the definition cards...and so on and so forth.
- Pictures
  - Of the item being reviewed
  - Or related to the concept being reviewed
  - Or mnemonic pictures to form an association

Instructions

1. Break down what they have to memorize into three related concepts, facts, pictures, meanings, etc.
2. Each card should contain one 'item'. (See example below)

el·e·phant | An enormous mammal with a very long nose called a trunk.

3. Label the back of each card in a set with a number so children can turn the card over and self-correct.

For example:

The word elephant, the picture of the elephant and the definition of the elephant would all be numbered #1 on the back.

The word zebra, the picture of the zebra and the definition of the zebra would all be numbered #2, etc.

Hint: Children can make these sets from photocopied masters. See examples of sample masters on the next few pages. They are made with a word processor on the computer using the "table" function. Children simply cut and paste the items on index cards.

Some children simply do not have legible handwriting. I recommend against forcing children to handwrite the cards unless they can print them clearly and legibly without taking an unreasonable amount of time to do the work. Cards must be printed for greatest memory retention. Avoid cursive.

Options for use:

- Children can match the cards on their own as a review.
- Children can pair up with a partner to match the cards.

Research indicates that we learn the most when we teach others. When two people work together to study, they are teaching each other.

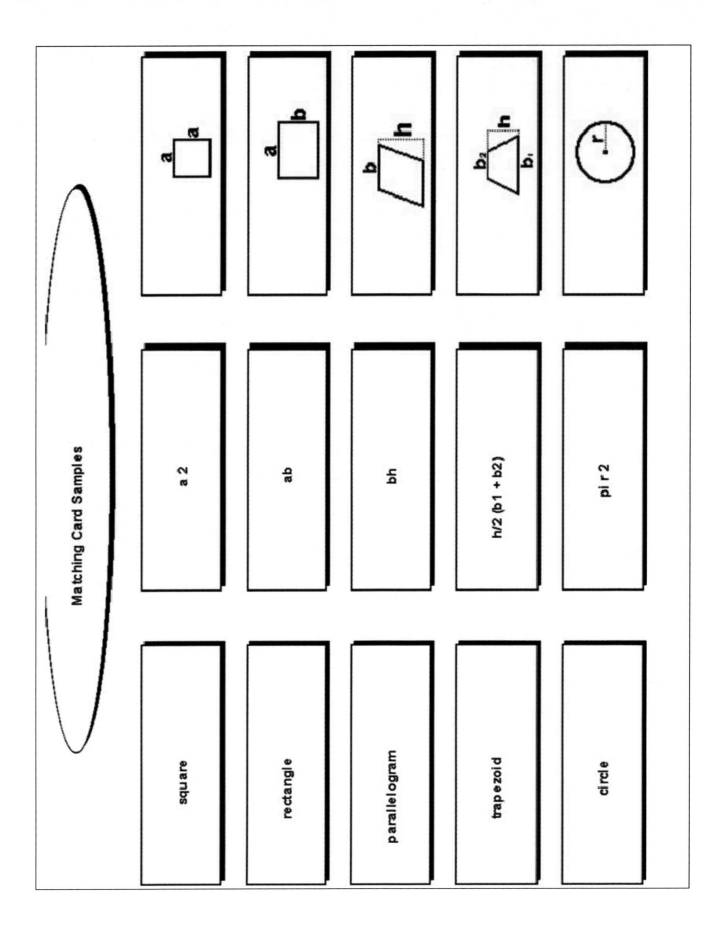

Matching Card Samples

Shape	Formula variable	Name
$\begin{array}{c}a\\a\end{array}$	a^2	square
$\begin{array}{c}b\\a\end{array}$	ab	rectangle
b h	bh	parallelogram
b_2 h b_1	h/2 (b1 + b2)	trapezoid
r	pi r 2	circle

Word	Visual	Definition
Folium of Descartes		x^3 + y^3 == 3x*y
Piriform		Parametric: {1,Sin[t]/h} * (1+Cos[t]). Period is 2 π.
el·e·**ph**ant		An enormous mammal with a very long nose called a trunk. They have curved tusks, huge, floppy ears, and four long, thick legs.

Ze-bra		A large mammal with a striped coat, long legs, and hooves. They are closely related to horses but have shorter manes.
Mam-mal		Warm-blooded animal with fur or hair on its skin and a skeleton inside its body.
cell		A tiny unit of plant or animal life, having a nucleus and surrounded by a very thin membrane.
mi-to-chon-dria		Any of the very tiny rod like or string like structures that occur in nearly all cells of plants and animals, and that process food for energy.

Word	Visual	Definition
nu · cle · us		The part of a cell that contains chromosomes, which control growth and reproduction in most living things.
Pla-teau		A high level area of land.
Val-ley		A long area of low land between mountains or hills. A stream or river often runs through a valley.
Word	Visual	Definition

"I don't know what to write!"

Clustering Activity

The clustering activity detailed on the following pages helps young children writing an essay through young adults filling out college applications.

Clustering Activity Step One

a. If your child has to write a paper, instruct him/her to draw a big circle on a piece of paper.

b. Put the topic of the paper in the center of the circle. Note: If there is more than one topic, you might have more than one circle: Writing about three wishes will require three circles: One for each wish.

c. Instruct your child to write any thoughts, ideas, and feelings about the topic in the circle. One can also ask questions about the topic or draw pictures of ideas.

d. Do not worry about spelling, grammar, sentences, etc. at this point. The purpose is to get the ideas out. Worry about writing rules later.

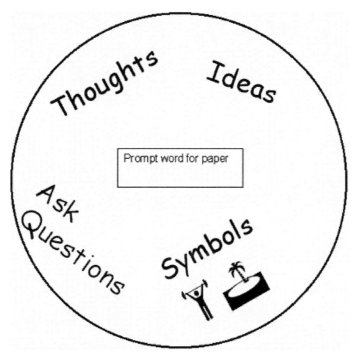

Make this circle BIG. At least the size of an 8" X 8" piece of paper.

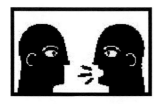

e. After your child "creates" in the circle, allow him or her to share what he or she has written with you.

Clustering Step Two

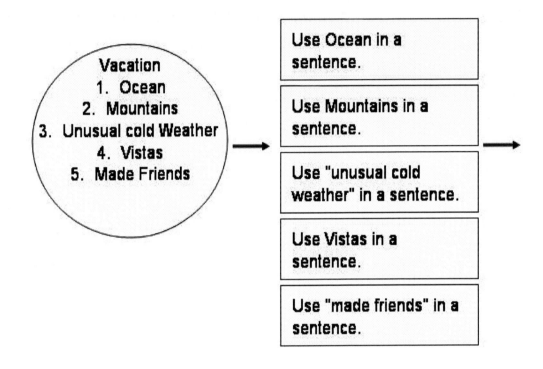

a. Instruct your child to take the "best" words and ideas from inside his/her circle and use each word in a sentence.

b. This is the topic sentence for the paragraphs he or she will write.

c. Write the sentences on strips of lined notepaper or lined sticky Post It notes.

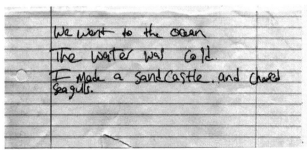

Clustering Step Three

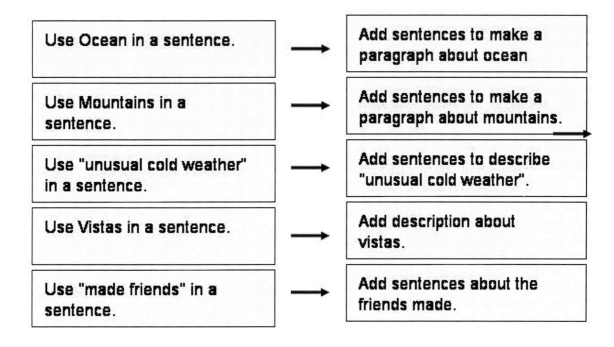

a. Now, take each sentence and add some more sentences about the topic sentence on that strip of paper.
b. Try to write two or three more sentences about the topic sentence.

*NOTE: Do not worry about spelling, grammar, or punctuation at this point in the exercise. Worrying about the rules makes it more difficult to be creative.

Clustering Step Four

Add sentences to make a paragraph about ocean	**Add Introduction**
Add sentences to make a paragraph about mountains.	
Add sentences to describe "unusual cold weather".	Add
Add description about vistas.	
Add sentences about the friends made.	**Add Conclusion**

Next, add an introduction and conclusion on separate strips of lined paper.

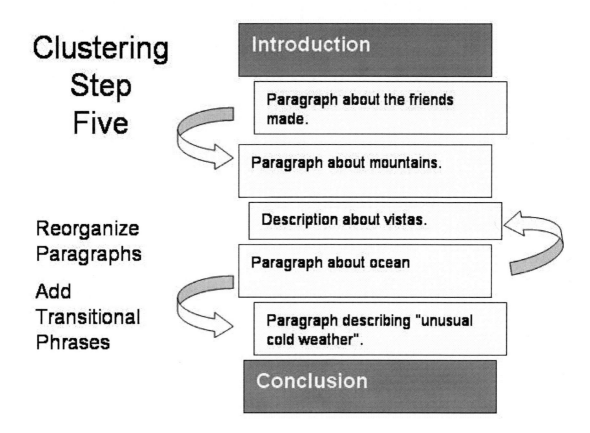

Clustering Step Five

Reorganize Paragraphs

Add Transitional Phrases

Introduction

Paragraph about the friends made.

Paragraph about mountains.

Description about vistas.

Paragraph about ocean

Paragraph describing "unusual cold weather".

Conclusion

a. Next, move the strips of paper around so that the paper is in the best order and makes the most sense.

b. This process allows the writer to start anywhere in the paper. It frees up creative thought and encourages the process to start. Organizing the paper after paragraphs are written is easy.

c. Scotch tape all the strips on one or two big pieces of paper.

d. Add transition words to make the paragraphs flow together

Examples of Transition Words:

To Add:

And, again, and then, besides, equally important, finally, further, furthermore, nor, too, next, lastly, what's more, moreover, in addition, first (second, etc.),

To Compare:
Whereas, but, yet, on the other hand, however, nevertheless, on the other hand, on the contrary, by comparison, where, compared to, up against, balanced against, but, although, conversely, meanwhile, after all, in contrast, although this may be true

To Prove:
Because, for, since, for the same reason, obviously, evidently, furthermore, moreover, besides, indeed, in fact, in addition, in any case, that is

To Show Exception:
Yet, still, however, nevertheless, in spite of, despite, of course, once in a while, sometimes

To Show Time:
Immediately, thereafter, soon, after a few hours, finally, then, later, previously, formerly, first (second, etc.), next, and then

To Repeat:
In brief, as I have said, as I have noted, as has been noted,

To Emphasize:
definitely, extremely, obviously, in fact, indeed, in any case, absolutely, positively, naturally, surprisingly, always, forever, perennially, eternally, never, emphatically, unquestionably, without a doubt, certainly, undeniably, without reservation

To Show Sequence:
First, second, third, and so forth. A, B, C, and so forth. next, then, following this, at this time, now, at this point, after, afterward, subsequently, finally, consequently, previously, before this, simultaneously, concurrently, thus, therefore, hence, next, and then, soon

To Give an Example:
For example, for instance, in this case, in another case, on this occasion, in this situation, take the case of, to demonstrate, to illustrate, as an illustration, to illustrate

To Summarize or Conclude:
In brief, on the whole, summing up, to conclude, in conclusion, as I have shown, as I have said, hence, therefore, accordingly, thus, as a result, consequently, on the whole

Clustering Step Six

Rewrite or type into one continuous draft on full sheets of paper.

Hand in draft for teacher to correct.

Introduction
Paragraph about the friends made.
Paragraph about mountains.
Description about vistas.
Paragraph about ocean
Paragraph describing "unusual cold weather".
Conclusion

If the teacher is not correcting a draft, you might help your child with this step.

Clustering Step Seven

Student writes final draft incorporating teacher corrections, feedback and edits.

My Vacation

By Successful Student

Interesting new friends became the focal point of ....

The mountains were...

The vistas were inspiring as mountains met the ocean in a clash of green and aquamarine...

Unfortunately there was an unusual cold weather front....

Overall, the vacation was...

This is the place where the student uses the rules and makes sure that spelling, grammar, and punctuation are correct.

Method for Writing Better Sentences

Simple Sentence:

_____

Are there any words that can be made more specific?

_____

Who?	What?	When?	Where?	Why?

New improved sentence:

_____.

_____.

Is there another way this sentence could begin?

_____.

_____.

Math Writing Tip for Spatial Difficulties

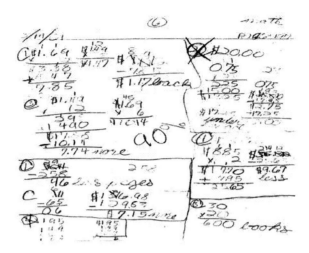

Are you tired of seeing math problems all jumbled up on an unlined piece of paper? Does it cause your child to make mistakes because numbers and equations are not lined up properly? Here is a simple solution!

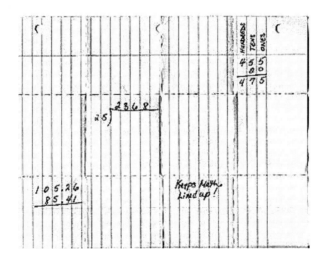

a. Keep math lined up!
b. Fold paper so that when you unfold it the paper is sectioned into squares. See picture above.
c. Turn standard lined paper sideways.
d. Grid paper also works very well. Make your own grid paper using the "Insert Table" function of your word processor.

Highlighting Activity

Put Prompts on Materials (or teach students to do it)

■ Simple prompts on materials can help students succeed.

 Star at the starting point.

Arrow to indicate direction.

𝒮𝑇𝒜𝑅𝑇 𝐻𝐸𝑅𝐸 ✓ Green mark to keep going

◉ **Bullets**

This is a strategy to teach children how to dissect and highlight an assignment so they "remember" all the parts.

When reviewing a homework assignment with your child, use highlighters and color markers to dissect the information on the assignment.

These prompts are presented in different colors. The simple act of picking up different color highlighters or markers works to keep children involved and attentive.

Post-It Note Method of "Highlighting"

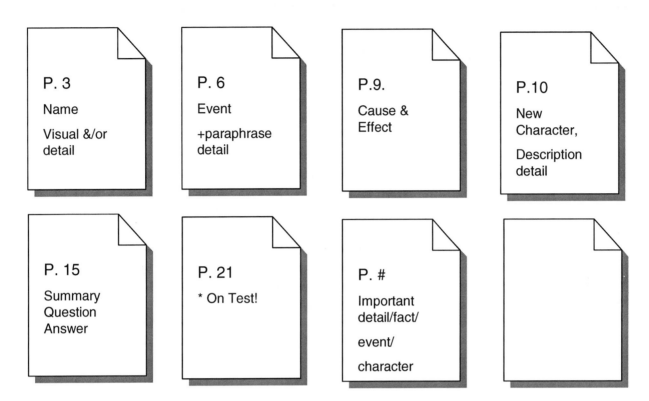

P. 3

Name

Visual &/or detail

P. 6

Event

+paraphrase detail

P.9.

Cause & Effect

P.10

New Character,

Description detail

P. 15

Summary Question Answer

P. 21

* On Test!

P. #

Important detail/fact/

event/

character

As students are reading a text, every time an important fact, item, cause and effect situation, etc., comes up, have students put a post-it note right in that spot and write the page number, the item and a visual or some detail.

After the chapter is read, the novel is finished, the text section is done, children should take all the post-it notes and line them up sequentially (as in the picture above) on a sheet of 8 ½ X 11 paper.

• Place the paper in a sleeve protector.
• Children now have a study guide that is tied to the text.

Draw It So You'll Know It

- Have your children draw pictures of what they are reading.
- Have youth illustrate their notes with drawings that represent what is in the notes.

This drawing is actually done in color markers. All pictures used in this handbook were originally done in color.

Sometimes current events are assigned and students must write about what they have read. For some learners this is a very vague assignment that brings tears and the exclamation, "I don't know what to write!" Use the current event form in this section to complete the current event assignment.

If the teacher has assigned a specific format for the way the current event should look for his/her class either:
- Ask the teacher if he/she will accept this completed form instead.
- Use this form as a way to structure the assignment and gather the information. Then re-write it in the required format.

Book Reports are often another source of frustration for students. Use the form here to gather the information required for the book report. There are prompts in the form that help the young person understand what different terms mean.

If the teacher has assigned a specific format for the way the book report should look for his/her class either:
- Ask the teacher if he/she will accept this completed form instead.
- Use this form as a way to structure the assignment and gather the information. Then re-write it in the required format.

Current Event Form

Circle one: World   Nation   Local

Do this: Find an article from a newspaper that is interesting to you. Answer the following questions about the article. Attach the article or a photocopy.

Who is the story about? (Your answer could be a group of people, an organization, or one person). _____

What event or happening does the article tell about?

_____
_____
_____
_____

Where did this event happen? (A city, a state, a building, or an area).

_____
_____

When did the event reported on in the article take place? (Time, a specific day or date, or a reference to a time-yesterday, last week, etc.).

_____
_____

Why did the event in the article happen? (Does your story explain what may have caused this to happen?)

_____
_____

What is your opinion about this article?

_____
_____
_____

Book Report

Title of Book:

_____

Author:

_____

Illustrator:

_____

Publishing Co.:

_____

Copyright date:

_____

Type of Story: Mystery, historical fiction, science fiction, adventure, biography,

TIME:

Historical period: (Medieval age, Victorian age, Early America, 1900's, etc.)

_____

Duration: (Over what period of time does the story take place? One day, several weeks, one hundred years, etc.?)

_____

PLACE:

Geographical location:

_____

Scenes: (Where does most of the story take place? Examples: outdoors, in someone's home, in a magician's castle)

_____

MAIN CHARACTER:

Name:

_____

Physical description :(What does he/she look like?)

_____

_____

_____

Personality description: (What makes him/her special?)

_____

_____

_____

How does this character change during the story?

_____

_____

_____

What feelings does he/she go through?

_____

_____

THE CONFLICTS IN THE STORY (The conflicts are the problems or hard decisions that the characters had to make)

CONFLICTS/PROBLEMS	HOW DID YOUR CHARACTER DEAL WITH THE PROBLEMS?
1	

CONFLICTS/PROBLEMS	HOW DID YOUR CHARACTER DEAL WITH THE PROBLEMS?
2	

CONFLICTS/PROBLEMS	HOW DID YOUR CHARACTER DEAL WITH THE PROBLEMS?
3	

TELL SOME OF THE EXCITING THINGS THAT YOUR CHARACTER DID AND HOW HIS OR HER PERSONALITY MADE THESE PARTS EXCITING.

_____

_____

_____

YOUR OPINION OF THIS STORY:

What did you like about it?

_____

_____

_____

_____

What didn't you like about it?

_____

_____

_____

_____

Homework Study Tools & Organizers

Studies indicate that when students keep track of their grades, their grades go up. One step better: Have your child keep track of all grades on the Grade Review Sheet, and then graph the grades in a bar graph.

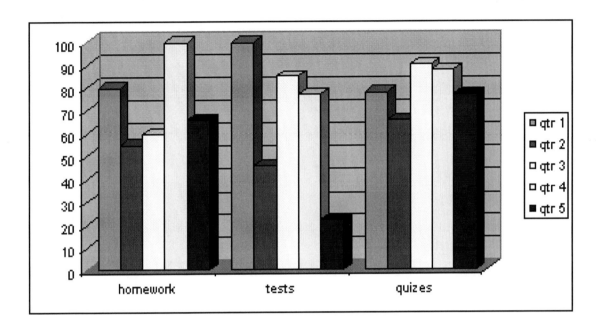

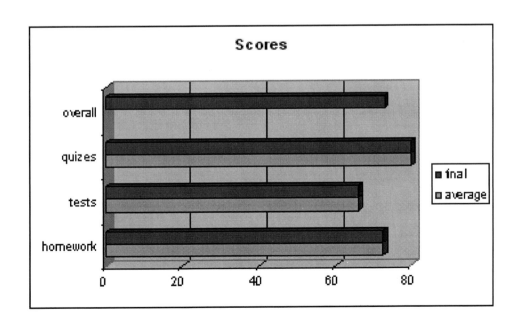

Team Name: _____   Quarter: _____

Grade Review Sheet

Name: _____   Class: _____

ASSIGNMENT	HW	CW	QUIZZES	TESTS
TITLE, DATE, GRADE	%	%	%	%

- Include DATE, TITLE AND GRADE for each assignment received.
- This grade list should be kept in the front of your binder!
- Graph your grades so you can SEE how you are doing! Use a bar or line graph.

Writing Tool: Portable Text Editor

 There are a few portable text editors on the market currently. Compare capability, cost, and adaptability to your situation. One example is the AlphaSmart 3000, a simple, portable, and affordable computer companion. It is compatible with any computer, Macintosh or PC, and with most printers. It enables users to type, edit, and electronically store text (for example, reports, essays, email messages or notes), and to practice keyboarding, without having to be at a computer. The text can then be transferred to any computer for formatting, or directly to a printer. Its portability allows children to use it anywhere and anytime (for example, in the classroom, at home or on field trips). The AlphaSmart has an optional 100% error-free IR (infrared) interface that allows wireless transfer between the AlphaSmart and a computer or printer.

Mandalas as a Tool to Focus, Calm and Get Creative

Mandala: a geometric or pictorial design usually enclosed in a circle

- Working from the center to the edge: Broadens attention
- Working from the edge to center: Focuses attention
- Relaxes the body
- Activates the Right Brain
- Visual Prompt/structural map for writing feelings in a poem, song or composition
- "Tilt the brain so language comes out differently" –Caryn Mirriam-Goldberg author of "Write Where you are" Free Spirit Press

A source for mandalas can be found at http://www.mandali.com/

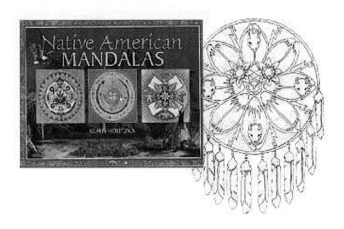

Offer Mandalas to your child if he/she is stressed, having difficulty with a writing assignment, or simply needs to calm down and get ready to work.

Color Your Own Mandala

- Sample from Monique Mandali , *Everyone's Mandala Coloring Book*, *http://www.mandali.com/*

Problem Solving Mind Map

Your young person comes to you with a problem and asks for your help to solve it. The problem solving form on the next page gives you a structure to discuss the problem.

For example, John comes home and complains that Chris is picking on him. He wants to beat Chris up.

- Take out the form and lay out the problem.
- In the top section write: Chris is picking on me.

- **Go to the first column. Where it says possible solution write:**
- Beat Chris up.
- Do not make a value judgment.
- List the pros/benefits of beating Chris up.
- List the cons/disadvantages (negative consequences) of beating Chris up.

- **Consider another solution:** Talking things out with Chris
- Go to the second column. Where it says possible solution write:
- Talk it out
- Do not make a value judgment.
- List the pros/benefits of talking it out.
- List the cons/disadvantages (negative consequences) of talking it out.

- **Continue brainstorming other options and follow the process.**

Now, John can be encouraged to make the best choice for him: One that has the most benefit and the least negative consequence.

This process can be used to make any decisions or solve many different problems.

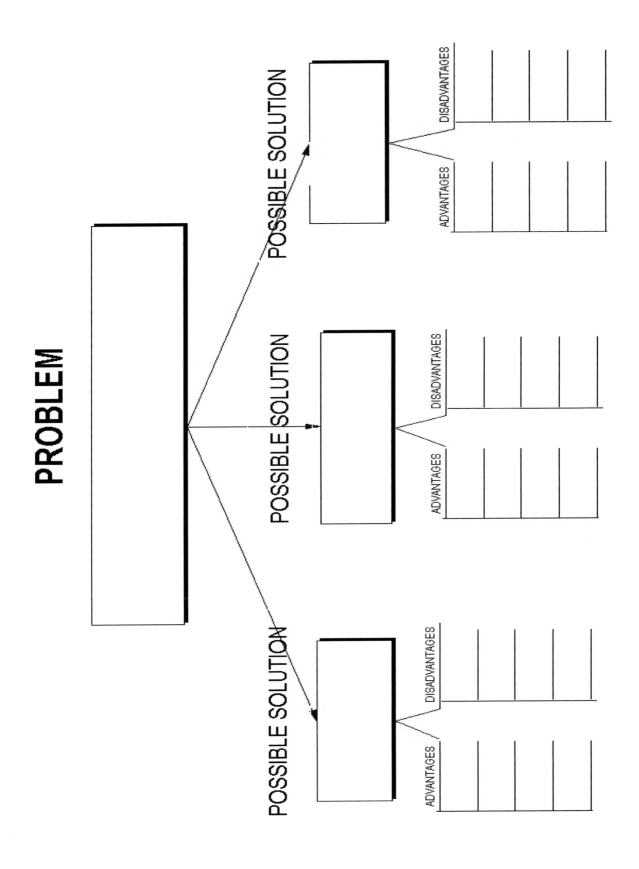

Organizing All That School Paperwork

Landmark Notebook System Materials List

The Landmark Notebook System is designed to help you keep your papers, assignments, handouts, etc. organized and in a location where you can find them should you need to refer to them again. Like any new system, it requires practice and discipline until it becomes a habit.

You will need:

- [ ] One 2" binder. You can put two subjects in one binder. (Four subjects required two binders)
- [ ] Portable three-hole punch
- [ ] Zippered pouch with holes to fit in binder
- [ ] A ruler with 3 holes
- [ ] 8-section dividers/binder
- [ ] Two three-hole divider pockets
- [ ] Two highlighters of different colors
- [ ] Post it notes
- [ ] Small Package of skinny colored markers or gel pens
- [ ] Highlighter tape
- [ ] Pens and pencils
- [ ] Three hole reinforcers
- [ ] One accordion file for each subject in a binder
- [ ] Assignment calendar/notebook

Set up your binder this way:

Work from the front and put in pieces in the following order:

- Three hole punch
- Ruler
- Zippered pouch with highlighters, writing utensils, tape, reinforcers, etc.
- Assignment calendar
- Divider labeled HOMEWORK
- Divider labeled NOTES
- Divider Labeled TESTS/QUIZZES
- Divider Labeled HANDOUTS
- Pocket Divider
- Repeat Dividers for second subject

1. Use sections for homework, notes, tests/quizzes, handouts for one lesson chapter/unit.

2. When the unit is finished, move ALL the papers to your accordion file for that subject and label that section with the unit name.

3. Save the accordion file at home for midterms and final exams. Do not throw study materials away!

For more information, contact Landmark Foundation @ 508-927-4440, www.landmarkschool.org

Add Checkboxes:

Draw checkboxes next to each step of an assignment to help your child remember to do all the steps. Check them off after they are complete. Example below:

NAME_____ PER_____DATE_____

CONSTELLATION PROJECT CHECKLIST

CHECK OFF EACH ITEM AS YOU COMPLETE IT!

☐ **Look up the constellation in a book. (There are books in the library and the science class)**

☐ **Draw the pattern of the stars that make it up.**

> A. Use plain white paper.
> B. Use BLACK ink or pencil.
> C. Make it no LARGER than 3 ½ " (height) X 8" (length).

☐ Connect the star patterns with DASHED lines.

☐ Cut out your constellations and mount it on BLACK construction paper at the TOP of the sheet.

☐ Pierce PIN HOLES (not massive holes) through the stars.

☐ Look up the myth about your constellation.

☐ Write the story (myth) in YOUR OWN WORDS.

☐ The final draft should be in PEN on plain WHITE PAPER.

☐ State where the myth comes from.

☐ Mount the myth BELOW your constellation on the black construction paper. (8 ½" X 11").

Use Microsoft Word Readability Statistics to Improve Writing

If students know what the readability level of their writing is, they can challenge themselves to bring it up higher! Simply use words with more syllables and write longer sentences that are more complex. Then spell check again and see if your reading level is higher!

To display readability statistics in MSWord (These instructions are for MSWord 2000):

- On the Tools menu, click Options, and then click the Spelling & Grammar tab.
- Select the *Check grammar with spelling* check box.
- Select the *Show readability statistics check box*, and then click OK.
- Click *Spelling and Grammar* on the Standard toolbar.
- When Word finishes checking spelling and grammar, it displays information about the reading level of the document.

TIP:

When copying and pasting text from Internet web sites into Microsoft Word:

1. Edit/Copy then highlight text from the website.
2. Go to your MSWord document
3. Click on Edit then choose PASTE SPECIAL
4. Paste as Formatted or Unformatted text, NOT HTML.

Now you can work with the information without the interference of invisible web code.

Acknowledgment
Dr. Mary S. Neumann, DHAP, NCHSTP, "Developing Effective Educational Print Materials"

In Word Perfect: To view the readability of a document
1   Click Tools Grammatik.
2   Click Options Analysis Readability.
3   In the Readability dialog box, choose a comparison document from the Comparison document list box.

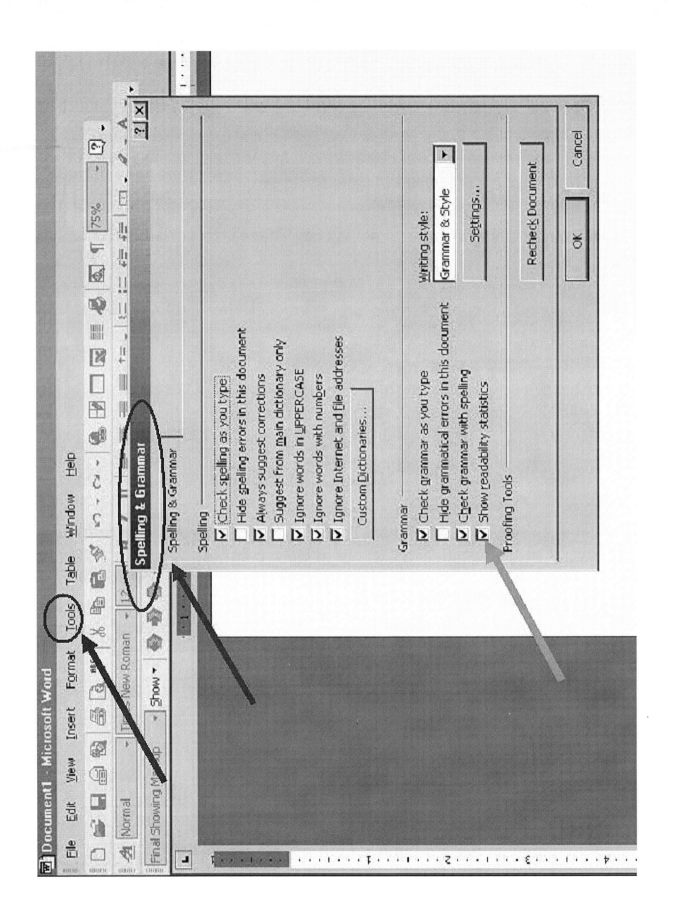

AutoSummarize in MSWord

Use AutoSummarize to highlight key points, create an abstract or a summary of your writing.

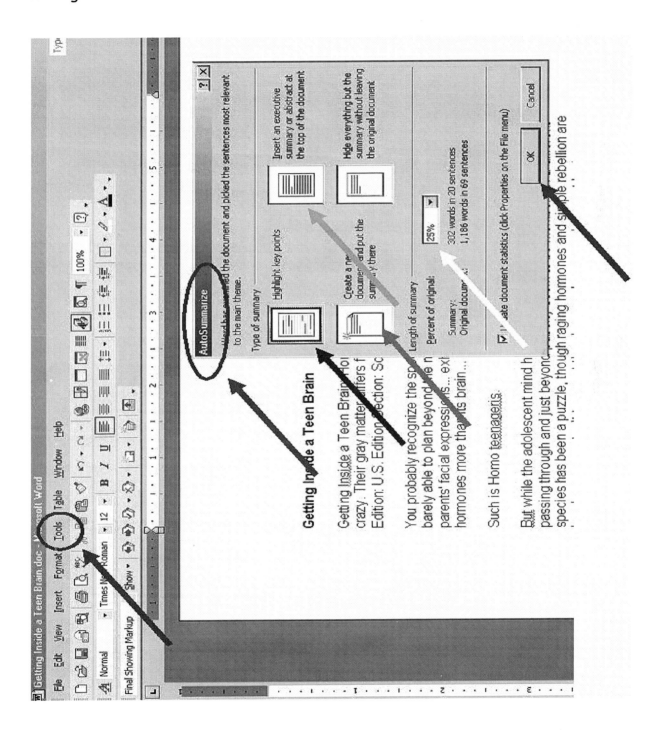

APPENDIX – RESOURCE LISTS

Books and Resource Articles

BEHAVIOR MANAGEMENT
Fitzell, Susan

- <u>Free The Children: Conflict Education for Strong Peaceful Minds,</u> New Society Publishers, 1997

Glasser, William, MD

- <u>Control Theory,</u> New York: Harper & Row, Inc., 1984
- <u>Reality Therapy,</u> New York: Harper & Row, Inc., 1975
- <u>Schools Without Failure,</u> New York: Harper & Row, Inc., 1975

Good, E. Perry

- <u>In Pursuit of Happiness: Knowing What You Want, Getting What You Need,</u> New View Publications, 1987

BRAIN BASED LEARNING
Caine, Geoffrey, & Caine, Renate Nummela & Crowell, Sam.

- <u>Mindshifts: A brain-based process for restructuring schools and renewing education.</u> Tucson, AZ: Zephyr Press. 1994
- <u>Making connections: Teaching and the human brain.,</u> Alexandria, VA: Association for Supervision and Curriculum Development. 1991

Jensen, Eric

- <u>Brain-Based Learning,</u> Turning Point Publishing, 1996
- <u>Brain Compatible Strategies,</u> Turning Point Publishing, 1997
- <u>Teaching with the Brain in Mind,</u> ASCD, 1998
- <u>The Great Memory Book,</u> The Brain Store, 1999

Greenleaf, Dr. Robert K

- <u>Brain Based Teaching: Building Excitement for Learning, 2000 Edition complete with applications</u>
- The Power of Two
- The Question,
  - ➤ To order Call 401-782-8507

Sylvester, Robert

- <u>A Celebration of Neurons: An Educators Guide to the Human Brain,</u> ASCD, 1995

COOPERATIVE LEARNING
Putnam, JoAnne W

- <u>Cooperative Learning and Strategies for Inclusion: Celebrating Diversity in the Classroom,</u> Paul H. Brookes,

---

COOPERATIVE LEARNING

1993 ISBN 1-55766-134-0

BRAIN COMPATIBLE APPROACH

Lewis, Barbara
- <u>The Kids Guide to Social Action</u>, Free Spirit Press, 1991

DiSpezio, Michael
- *Critical Thinking Puzzles*, Sterling Publishers, ISBN 0-8069-9430-4 (Mnemonics)

LEARNING DISABILITIES

Bell, Nancy and Lindamood, Phyllis
- <u>Vanilla Vocabulary</u>, Academy of Reading Publications, 1993

Heacox, Diane
- <u>Up From Underachievement</u>, Free Spirit Press, 1991

Rief, Sandra and Heimburge, Julie
- <u>How To Reach & Teach All Students In The Inclusive Classroom.</u> The Center for Applied Research, 1996

Sedita, Joan
- <u>Landmark Study Skills Guide</u> Landmark Foundation, Call (508) 927-4440 Ext. 2116, www.landmark.pvt.k12.ma.us/landmark

Schumm, Jeanne Shay and Yddencich, Marguerite
- <u>School Power</u>, Free Spirit Press, 1992 (This book is a gold mine for providing photo-copyable forms for students to organize writing and reports.)

Tomlinson Carol Ann
- <u>The Differentiated Classroom</u> ISBN: 0-87120-342-1

Winebrenner, Susan
- <u>Teaching Kids with Learning Difficulties in the Regular Classroom: Strategies and Techniques Every Teacher Can Use To Challenge & Motivate Struggling Students</u>, Free Spirit Publishing, 1996

Friend, Marilyn and Bursuck, William D.
- <u>Including Students with Special Needs: A Practical Guide for Classroom Teachers, 3/e</u>, Publisher: Allyn & Bacon, Copyright: 2002Format: Paper, 544 pp <u>ISBN:</u> <u>0-205-33192-0</u>

MULTIPLE INTELLIGENCES

Armstrong, Thomas
- <u>Multiple Intelligences In The Classroom</u>, ASCD, 1994

Armstrong, Thomas
- <u>Multiple Intelligences In The Classroom</u>, Association for Supervision & Curriculum Development; ISBN: 0871203766; 2nd edition (May 15, 2000)

Gardner, Howard.
- <u>Frames of mind: The Theory of Multiple Intelligences.</u> (Paperback ed.). Basic Books, 1985

MULTIPLE INTELLIGENCES

* The Unschooled Mind: How Children Think and How Schools Should Teach. Basic Books, 1991

Gibbs, Jeanne

* Tribes: A New Way of Learning and Being Together, Center Source, 1987

Lazear, David

* Seven Ways of Teaching, Skylight Publishing, Inc., 1991

PEER TUTORING

Ashley, W., J. Jones, G. Zahniser, and L. Inks.

* Peer Tutoring: A Guide To Program Design. Research and Development Series No. 260. Columbus: Ohio State University Center for Research in Vocational Education, 1986. ED 268 372.

Bloom, B.

* "The Search for Methods of Group Instruction as Effective One-to-One Tutoring." EDUCATIONAL LEADERSHIP 41 (1984): 4-17.

Cohen, P.

* "Outcomes of Tutoring." AMERICAN EDUCATIONAL RESEARCH JOURNAL 19 (1982): 237-248.

Crushon, I.

* Peer Tutoring: A Strategy For Building On Cultural Strengths. Documentation and Technical Assistance In Urban Schools, 1977. ED 228 367.

PERSONALITY TYPES

Lawrence, Gordon

* People Types & Tiger Stripes, CAPT, Inc. 1996

Silver, Strong and Perini

* So Each May Learn: Integrating Learning Styles and Multiple Intelligences, ASCD. 2000

TEST BIAS & GRADING

Berk, R.A. (Ed.).

* "Handbook of methods for detecting test bias." Baltimore, MD: The Johns Hopkins Univ.Press.1982

Estrin, Elise Trumbull

* Alternative Assessment: Issues in Language, Culture, and Equity, 1993 http://equity.enc.org/equity/eqtyres/erg/104176/4176.htm

Munk, Dennis & Bursuck, William

* Report Card Grading Adaptations for Students with Disabilities: Types and Acceptability, Intervention in School & Clinic, 1 May 1998

Munk, Bursuck, & Olson

* The Fairness of Report Card Grading Adaptations:

TEST BIAS & GRADING

What Do Students With and Without Learning Disabilities Think?, Remedial & Special Education, 1 Mar 1999.

Produced by the ASPIIRE and ILIAD IDEA Partnerships in cooperation with the U.S. Department of Education.

- Making Assessment Accommodations: A Toolkit for Educators, Video captioned in English and Spanish. 2000, 146 pages. 14 minutes. ISBN 0-86586-3644, Council For Exceptional Children, #P5376 $99.00/CEC Members $69.00

VISUAL ORGANIZERS

Buzan, Tony

- The Mind Map[6] Book. ISBN 0 563 86373 8, 1993.

Booher, Dianna.

- Clean Up Your Act; Effective Ways to Organize Paperwork and Get It Out of Your Life

Haber, Ralph N

- "How We Remember What We See". Scientific America, 105, May 1970.

Margulies, Nancy

- Mapping Inner Space: Learning and Teaching Mind Mapping

Rico Lusser, Gabriele

- Writing The Natural Way ISBN: 0-87477-186-2 and 0-87477-236-s (ppbk.)

---

[6] "Mind Map" is a registered trademark of the Buzan Organization 1990.

Catalogues for Recorded Book Loans, Rentals and Sales

Audio books combine important ingredients in creating a successful lifelong reader. Audio books:

- Motivate students to read
- Allow students to enjoy a book at their interest level that might be above their reading level
- Allow slower readers to participate in class activities
- Provide a way to learn the patterns of language, learn expressions, and increase vocabulary.
- Are good examples of fluent reading for children, young adults and for people learning English as a second language.
- Builds the neural connections necessary for auditory processing skills. Auditory processing skills are required for literacy.
- Improves listening skills
- For pre-reading, it familiarizes students with the story so that students can concentrate on the words when they read the text.
- Bring a book to life thereby inspiring, entertaining and linking language and listening to the reading experience.
- Build a reading scaffold--broadening vocabularies, stretching attention spans, flexing thinking skills

1. Recorded Book Rentals (800) 638-1304 Telephone
2. Books on Tape (800) 626-3333 Telephone
3. Chivers Audio Books (800) 621-0182 Telephone
4. Blackstone Audiobooks (800) 729-2665 Telephone
5. The Teaching Company (800) 832-2412 Telephone
6. Sells taped lectures on history, literature, etc. Ask to hear their free sample lecture on "How to Understand and Listen to Great Music", one of a series of 16 lectures on music.
7. Recording for the Blind & Dyslexic (800) 221-4792 Telephone
8. They have 75,000 unabridged books on tape. They also sell portable four track cassette players ($99 – $199). Students can get textbooks custom-recorded; ask for information. Fees are $50.00 to apply and $25.00 per year thereafter—all the books you can read; no postage required. Application form includes a form for your doctor to sign.

World Wide Web Resources

The links below are also available online at
http://www.aimhieducational.com/inclusion_urls.html

Website URL	Topic	Category
http://www.aimhieducational.com/inclusion.html	29 Positive Aspects of ADD/ADHD	ADD
http://www.audioenhancement.com/ae/SiteDefault.aspx	Audio Enhancement	Auditory
http://www.sensorycomfort.com/	**Resources for ADD, Autism**	Autism
http://www.explosivechild.com	**The Explosive Child**	Behavior
http://www.explosivechild.com	Helping easily frustrated, inflexible children	Behavior
http://www.judyringer.com	Making More Powerful Choices	Behavior
http://www.ldonline.org/ld_indepth/teaching_techniques/strategy_cards.html	Using Strategy Cards to Enhance Cooperative Learning for Students with Learning Disabilities	Behavior
http://www.wglasser.com/	William Glasser Institute	Behavior
http://www.aimhieducational.com/books/spedbooks.html	Brain Gym Resources	Brain
http://www.aimhieducational.com/inclusion.html	Brain Research Sheds New Light on Student Learning, Teaching Strategies, and Disabilities	Brain
http://www.brainconnection.com	Brain Based Learning site	Brain
http://www.brains.org/hottopics.htm	Hot Topics in Current Research	Brain
http://www.cainelearning.com/pwheel/	The Brain/Mind Learning Principals	Brain
http://collabfab.com	Free tool to foster collaboration.	Collab
http://powerof2.org	Collaboration	Collab
http://www.ku-crl.org/archives/misc/hudson.html	Co-Teaching Resource	Collab
http://www.marilynfriend.com	Co-teaching, collaboration and grading	Collab
http://www.powerof2.org/	Resource site for collaborative teaching	Collab
http://www.eyeoneducation.com/newsletters/639-x.htm	Differentiated Instruction: A Guide for Middle and High School Teachers	DI
http://pss.uvm.edu/pss162/learning_styles.html	Learning styles Inventory- MI	Diversity
http://www.aimhieducational.com/inclusion.html	Imagine Teaching Robin Williams-Twice-Exceptional Children in Your School	Diversity
http://www.aimhieducational.com/inclusion.html	10 Resource Articles: Bilingual, ESL, Multicultural	Diversity
http://www.ginnyhoover.com/learning.htm	Learning Style Resource	Diversity
http://www.hots.org/	Poverty and Learning	Diversity
http://www.myersbriggs.org/applying/education.cfm	Using MBTI Type in Education	Diversity

URL	Description	Category
http://www.nldline.com/	Non-Verbal Learning Disorder	Diversity
http://www.pbs.org/wgbh/misunderstoodminds/	Misunderstood Minds	Diversity
http://www.weaverclinic.com/	Learning Style and attention issues	Diversity
http://www.hes-inc.com/hes.cgi/02120.html	The Teacher's Resource Guide (A strategy goldmine)	Ed Gen
http://www.teachersplanet.com/special.shtml	Teacher Resource	Ed Gen
http://www.teachervision.com	General Resource	Ed Gen
http://www.teachnology.com/	The Web Portal for Educators	Ed Gen
http://www.csun.edu/~vcecn006/	Writing Resource	English
http://depts.stcc.mass.edu/projectaccess/equipment.htm	List of Adaptive Equipment	Equip
http://theatrelighting.com/gel.html	**Theatrical Lighting Gel**	Equip
http://www.alphasmart.com/	AlphaSmart Text Editor	Equip
http://www.dryerase.com/	High Quality Dry Erase Boards	Equip
http://www.fullspectrumsolutions.com/index.html	Source for Full Spectrum Lighting	Equip
http://www.keyboardinstructor.com	Text Editor & Applications	Equip
http://www.stokespublishing.com	Teach Timer	Equip
http://www.hardin.k12.ky.us/res_techn/sbjarea/math/JeopardyDirections.htm	**Jeopardy Game Directions**	Game
http://www.cec.sped.org/bk/catalog2/assessment.html	**Assessment Tool Kit**	Grading
http://www.fairtest.org/index.htm	National Center for Fair & Open Testing	Grading
http://www.newpaltz.edu/migrant/grading.html	Grading Students in Inclusive Settings	Grading
http://www.teachtci.com/default.asp	History Alive	History
http://currmap.ncrel.org/default.htm	Curriculum Mapping	How-to
http://www.help4teachers.com/	Layered Curriculum	How-to
http://www.humboldt.edu/~lfr1/kindling.html	Lesson Plan: Kindling - Making it Meaningful	How-to
http://www.aimhieducational.com/books/spedbooks.html	Books on Topics covered in seminar	Inclusion
http://www.aimhieducational.com/books/spedbooks.html	Paraprofessional's Guide to the Inclusive Classroom	Inclusion
http://www.inclusion.com/	Inclusion Resource	Inclusion
http://www.newhorizons.org/spneeds_intr.html	Inclusive Schools	Inclusion
http://www.quasar.ualberta.ca/ddc/incl/intro.htm#top	Inclusion: School as a Caring Community (Excellent Resource)	Inclusion
http://www.ualberta.ca/~jpdasddc/INDEX.html	Inclusion Resource	Inclusion
http://www.wrightslaw.com/	**Special Ed Law Advocates**	Law
http://tmwmedia.com/algebra_tutor.html	Algebra Tutor Video	Math
http://www.aimhieducational.com/books/spedbooks.html	Visual Math: See How Math Makes Sense	Math
http://www.aimhieducational.com/inclusion.html	Graphic Organizers	Math
http://www.dotolearn.com	Math grids and much more	Math
http://www.fasenet.org/store/kay_toliver/eddiefiles.html	Math Videos	Math
http://www.marcycookmath.com	Zip Around Cards, I have/Who has?	Math
http://www.mathgen.com/remedial.htm	Math Resource	Math
http://www.rogertaylor.com/	Click on Resource Library for Math Songs	Math
http://www.teachingideas.co.uk/maths/contents.htm	Math Ideas	Math

http://www.tsbvi.edu/math/index.htm	Teaching Math to visually impaired students	Math
http://www.aimhieducational.com/inclusion.html	Reading, Writing, Rapping	Music
http://www.jazzdigger.com/b/Ron_Brown/	Music to Teach by	Music
http://www.musicintheclassroom.com/	Music to Teach by	Music
http://www.neilslade.com	Music to Teach by	Music
http://www.rocknlearn.com/	Learning to Music	Music
http://www.shakeandlearn.com	**Grammar, math, science and language to music**	Music
http://www.songsforteaching.com/index.html	Music to Teach by	Music
http://www.applest.com/intelligear.asp	Intelli-Gear: Organizers & Learning Style	Org
http://www.homeworknow.com	Online homework resource	Org
http://www.landmarkschool.org/	Binder & Study Skills	Org
http://www.africana.com/research/encarta/tt_091.asp	Maya, Angelou	Other
http://www.lucidcafe.com/library/currentread/currentread04.html	Nikola Tesla	Other
http://www.nwrel.org/scpd/catalog/modellist.asp	List of Model Programs	Program
http://src.scholastic.com/ecatalog/readingcounts/lexiles/index.htm	Lexile Framework for Reading	Reading
http://www.scientificlearning.com/	Fast ForWord;Develops language & listening skills for reading.	Reading
http://www.sundancepub.com/c/@5RKYpnKw1bYvA/Pages/index.html	Reading Resource	Reading
http://school.discovery.com/schrockguide/assess.html	Rubrics	Rubrics
http://www.rubrics4teachers.com/	Rubrics	Rubrics
http://school.discovery.com	Science Resource	Science
http://www.ericfacility.net/ericdigests/ed433185.html	Science Classrooms for Students with Special Needs	Science
http://www.webelements.com/	Interactive Periodic Table	Science
http://www.readplease.com/	Reads any web page, makes mp3/wav files, zooms any page, text-only version web pages, translates and much more!	Software
http://www.cast.org/udl/index.cfm?i=211&option=Introduction	The software can take electronic text content from any source and read it using synthesized speech and visual highlighting.	Software
http://www.computerautomation.com/	Special Education Automation Software	Software
http://www.inspiration.com/	Graphic Organizer Software	Software
http://www.brainchild.com	**Online assessments of state tests**	Software & Tech
http://www.mimio.com	Interactive whiteboard technology	Software & Tech
http://www.disabilityresources.org/FAMOUS.html	Famous people with LD	SpEd
http://www.disabilityresources.org/index.html	Resource	SpEd
http://www.ideapractices.org/resources/index.php	**Professional Development Resources**	SpEd
http://www.iser.com/	LD Professional Directory	SpEd
http://www.ku-crl.org/iei/index.html	Ctr for Res'ch on Learning	SpEd

http://www.ldonline.org/	**LD Online Resource**	SpEd
http://www.lrpdartnell.com/cgi-bin/SoftCart.exe/scstore/01_Special_Ed/cat-IDEA.html?E+scstore	Special Education Products	SpEd
http://muskingum.edu/~cal/database/	Learning Strategies Database	strategy
http://www.aimhieducational.com/inclusion.html	Cut and Paste 101	strategy
http://education.umn.edu/NCEO/AccomStudies.htm	Online Accommodations bibliography	Tools
http://puzzlemaker.school.discovery.com/	Puzzlemaker	Tools
http://us.dk.com/?11CS^home	**Dorling Kindersley**	Tools
http://wikkistix.com	Hands on Learning, Figit Toys	Tools
http://www.aimhieducational.com/books/spedbooks.html	Mandala Coloring Books	Tools
http://www.aimhieducational.com/brainchild.html	Brainchild: Technology builds English & Math Mechanics in line with State Standards	Tools
http://www.epraise.com	Recognition Products & ideas	Tools
http://www.graphicorganizers.com/	**Graphic Organizers- many free samples**	Tools
http://www.mindbinders.com/	Mindbinders Study Cards (Those cute ones on a ring)	Tools
http://www.schoolhousetech.com/	Worksheet Factory	Tools
http://www.studygs.net/	Study guides and strategies	Tools
http://www.sunburstmedia.com/	For Language Learners	Tools
http://www.teachervision.fen.com/lesson-plans/lesson-6293.html	Graphic Organizers	Tools
http://www.thinkingmaps.com/	**Visual Teaching Tools**	Tools
http://www.trainerswarehouse.com	**Teacher & Presenter Supplies**	Tools
http://www.mindtools.com/memory.html	Tools for improving Memory	Tools
home.att.ne+t/~clnetwork/thinkps.htm	Think Pair Share Options	TPS
http://vischeck.com	**See what it's like to be color blind**	Visual
http://www.irlen.com/training_teacher.htm	How Teachers can help w/vision problems	Visual
http://www.nora.cc/index.html	Vision Issues Resource	Visual
http://www.oep.org/	**Behavioral Optometry**	Visual
http://www.pavevision.org	Parents Active for Vision Education	Visual
http://www.tsbvi.edu	Blind and Visually Impaired	Visual
http://www.vis-ed.com/	Visual Ed Study Card Sets	Visual
http://www.drawingwriting.com/index.html	Drawing/Writing and the new literacy	Writing
http://www.stepuptowriting.com/default.asp	Multisensory writing strategies	Writing

WORKSHOPS FOR PARENTS, PARENT EDUCATORS AND TEACHERS

Susan has successfully completed 21 hours of Parent Learning Network Parent Educator Training sponsored by the Texas Association of School Boards. She is trained to deliver workshops based on the *Family Frameworks* and *The Early Years* curricula. The curricula was written by the Texas Association of School Boards staff members in cooperation with content researchers across Texas.

The curricula units emphasize active learning techniques that empower participants to become their own problem solvers. The lesson plans offer activities that appeal to the multiple intelligences and promote learning the way the brain is best and biologically designed to learn. Participants will have an opportunity to share ideas, support each other, study current research, and work together as a team to find answers to their questions.

Workshop Topics

- Choices and Consequences: Bullying
- Finding Balance in Stressful Lives
- Parents & Schools Working Together
- Peer Pressure
- Please Help Me With My Homework!
- Understanding Yourself and Others: Keys to Better Relationships
- Why Won't Children Listen?

Program costs:
Costs are determined on an individual basis.

Contact information:
To schedule a consultation/ training or for more information, telephone 210-473-2863 from 7:00 a.m. EST through 8:00 p.m, EST, Monday through Friday . Fax: 210-473-2863.
E-mail: sfitzell@aimhieducational.com* www.aimhieducational.com

AIMHI Educational Programs

PO Box 6182
Manchester, NH 03108-6182

Phone: 603-625-6087
Fax: 603-625-6087
Email: sfitzell@aimhieducational.com

Purchase Order

Bill To: **Ship To:**

Purchase Order #:
Date:
Vendor ID:

Please PRINT your e-mail address clearly:

_____

Quantity	Item	Description	Retail Price	Discount % price	Total
		FREE THE CHILDREN: CONFLICT EDUCATION FOR STRONG, PEACEFUL MINDS by Susan Fitzell	15.95		
		SET OF 10		125.00	
		SPECIAL NEEDS IN THE GENERAL CLASSROOM: STRATEGIES TO MAKE IT WORK	19.00		
		SET OF 10		150.00	
		TRANSFORMING ANGER TO PERSONAL POWER: AN ANGER MANAGEMENT CURRICULUM GUIDE FOR GRADES 6-12	19.00		
		SET OF 10		150.00	
		PLEASE HELP ME WITH MY HOMEWORK! STRATEGIES FOR PARENTS AND CAREGIVERS	15.95		
		SET OF 10		100.00	
			Subtotal		
			Shipping and Handling		
			Total		

Shipping and Handling

1-5 books — mailed priority   4.00/book

5+ books add 10% to cover

Notes: